Notice

Copyright © 2019 Tyler Carrington Kernodle

Published by Tyler Carrington Kernodle

All rights reserved. This book or parts thereof may not be reproduced in any form, stored in any retrieval system, or transmitted in any form by any means—electronic, mechanical, photocopy, recording, or otherwise—without prior written permission of the publisher, except as provided by the United States of America copyright law. For permission requests, write to the publisher, at "Attention: Permissions Coordinator," at tckernodle@gmail.com.

Paperback ISBN: 978-0-359-94726-3

Printed by Lulu Press Inc. in the United States of America.

First printing, 2019.

Front cover image by Tyler Carrington Kernodle.

www.partshomegrown.com

plush

By Carrington Kernodle

This small book of poetry is dedicated to my family, my lover & my higher self.

TABLE OF CONTENTS

INTRO

BOOK 1: IN NATURE

BOOK 2: IN THE MIND

BOOK 3: IN LOVE

BOOK 4: IN RETROSPECT

OUTRO

INTRO

black rose oil

I learned how to
process down this aisle
probably around age two.
Yes, as a mere child.

"She's a doll!"
proclaimed a deaconess,
but I felt too small
to become an empress.

Today I stumbled upon,
a book from a faint memory,
of a spiritual bond
that made my eyes shimmery.

A few drops of anointing oil
signals high priesthood.
A single drop of black rose oil
means the second coming of womanhood.

BOOK ONE: IN NATURE

emerson

Sage charring

Rhythms pacing with the heart

Up the cavities

Innocence radiates throughout

A memoir comes

To mind starting with an acorn

Minute to most

Kicked down into the dirt alone

Drinking leftovers

Unbeknownst a development

In God's image

This manifestation confuses those

Unaware, unloved

A coming to be of a mahogany tree

Deeply rooted

In love with the process that made she.

bickering

The sunshine flickered

upon the lake.

Canaries snickered

for their own sake.

Beyond the evergreens

a prism beams.

So it must mean

a place this serene

is a mere dream.

    "Never rely on the senses"

    said the French man.

    "Notice when your heart tenses"

    said the good woman.

    Do I know when

    the earth breathes?

    It's when she pushes

        my curls aside

        moves the tide

        and tells my soul

        to no longer hide.

        "So stop bickering

        with yourself my child."

a sky's goodbye

Bothersome it's been

to witness the sky

mimic a sin.

A wrongdoing

unto the self.

A lack of pursuing

by myself.

Bothersome it's been

to witness the sky

when the sun sets in ten

since I

can't stand by

another goodbye

comprised of lies.

Bothersome it's been

to witness the sky

for we are too shy

for how hard we

are about to cry.

my place

Loneliness festers,
just oozing all over.

But suffocate those ears to hear
a place.

Yes, that place.
Where skin resembles the lake.

Where a moon so bent,
blue and black hues remain lit.

Soften the moss with thy flesh.
Let the water whisper on my chest.

Take a deep breath
and go deaf.

This is my place,
there is a lot to embrace.

rise & cry

Earth turned around

Sun pinches veils

Here lies you

Here you lied

Rippling refractions

Casting pass

Plain glass

Sanctified teeth grind

Tears off the towel

Collecting spilled milk

And the honey

Of honey

O' honey.

evergreen

Why can't I be

An evergreen?

I'd be very tall

And maybe less mean.

But I should be honest

And come clean.

About the true reason why

I have this dream.

My lover's eyes are

So green

Rarely from envy

Yet he still causes a scene.

I can't look away

From something so serene.

Hard to believe

He's just a human being.

For a soul like his

Can never be unseen.

It seems to have lived forever

Like a beautiful evergreen.

BOOK TWO: IN MIND

bad blood

Blood is thicker than water right?
More follows that recycled catchphrase.

O positive rushes
Under this skin.

"Be positive" shushes
Feelings toward my kin.

I'm ruining the pits of my sweater.
But this heart is growing cold.

Pleas go unheard.
Deeds overdone.

Like a caged bird,
My keeper already won.

The blood of the covenant
Is thicker than the water of the womb.

Blood read deep.
Water makes me weak.

strange.

Blinking harder

Deciphering how

As is

Why I am so strange.

Bubbles on

Ocean water

As is

Seems strange.

Air cusp with

Thin skin

Floating on the sea

Is considerably strange.

Meant to be under

Under pressure

To implode

Implode silently.

Is that what

I'm supposed to do?

That too

Is quite, I don't know, strange.

before the meeting.

Awkward posture.
Elevating the music to
Deafening heavens.
Fatigued at swatting.
Confused on breathing abilities.
There's no breeze.
No warmth from stars.
Chests and clouds move.
But nothing else seems to.
Better to be
Alone and alive or
Lonely and lied to.
My problem is
His problem is
Her problem is
Irrelevant.

stoplight

He was a bad driver.

The kind that
did illegal things
when nobody was around.

And just like
that stoplight,
one night,
he ran right through me.

pour

Its 7:01.
Pour over a thin filter
to steep the coffee.

Its 7:06.
Pour now through a thin tree line
sunshine to inside.

Its 7:08.
Pour from deep down to explore
how you are source-fed.

Its 7:19.
Pour water only knee high to
bathe in the shallow.

Its 7:40.
Pour some dirt from the soft earth
to grow what you've sown.

Its 8:31.
Pour your energy right here,
peace lives in you my dear.

homegrown

Home
is where I've flown
from the vast unknown.

Home
is where I've known
fruit from seeds sown.

Home
is where I'm shown
how to be my own.

Home
is where I've grown
to never feel alone.

BOOK THREE: IN LOVE

canelé

Young hearts as dainty
as a French pastry,
they finally met
at MarieBette.

While their imagination started to bloom,
feelings came in like a monsoon.
Cheeks filled with petite canelé,
they talked 'till end of day.

Barista yelled final call.
No longer could these two stall.
Knowing the moment would be missed,
goodbyes were given with a coffee stained kiss.

confrontation.

Stop.

  I can't.

    That's enough.

      Nobody is allowed

        To confront me

          Like that ok?

        Thanks.

          But.

            Come back.

          I need that.

              That feeling of my heart

            In whiplash.

              That soul to soul

                Pushback.

                  That if you don't answer me

                I'm not coming back.

                  For if I want this to be

                    The best love story

                      Then I need for you to keep

                    Confronting me.

what my intuition is yelling

His presence was of divine nature.

Flesh reminiscent of clay work

Carved yet smooth

Warm undertones.

No syllable

Poorly flows from

His mouth

For he is well intentioned.

See what my

Intuition is yelling

Is that he

Is the epitome

Of pure honey.

The kind from the comb

Back home.

I am at home.

He feels like home.

Eating too much

Speaking too soon

Gave me a toothache

But not a heartbreak.

Blessed I am

For meeting said man

Peace be onto me

Peace be onto he.

asterisk

How do you feel
about the stars?
I believe in them.

There's more
for you to know
and
there's a star
for me to show.
So here I go.

I love you.*

*unconditionally

honeymoon phase

I love you

To the moon

And back.

With you

There is no honeymoon

Phase that we lack.

Can you

Feel the full moon

On your skin like a tack?

Said by you

"Baby you bask under our moon"

And a smile began to crack.

All this love is for you

For no matter the phases of the moon

My heart will never turn blue black.

a day

A day of

relentless raining
cast-iron cooking
hums harmonizing
sofa squishing
flames flickering
bashful blinking
mind mingling
latte lulling
and
soul sharing

with him,
is a day well spent.

BOOK FOUR: IN RETROSPECT

carefree

My handwriting

is well, illegible.

But that's because

I think too fast.

Sink too fast.

Maybe I should

go on a fast?

The ones that

rid toxins.

I can fast!

Rid myself

of my self.

I can't fast.

Love myself

for my self.

I can care!

Free myself

from my self.

I don't care!

Please myself

with my self.

So anyways,

I write for myself.

table

I know what I bring to the table

So trust me,

I'm not eating alone.

misty's magnolia

3 years in a row
Magnolias
Ceased to exist
When I needed them most.

Not in season
Scrambled
With what to gift her
When asking for nothing.

So on the 11th of May
A box of turtles
Cursive inside a card
And my presence
Was all I could display.

I started to apologize
For lack of flowers
She lifted her hazel eyes
Interlocked, this moment was ours.

"You are my favorite flower, child.
Your scent is mild.
Your curls go wild.
Your path is already tiled
All because you are my child."

No longer did I feel Misty Blue.
That day, my love for her grew.

color

The sun bled
into a rich burgundy.

Soon merging with
this violent violet.

The framing was
navy with white freckles.

Trees swayed underneath
in a tinted green.

Clouds pillowed into
a marbled gray.

I could never have
One favorite color.

Not after seeing
All of that.

advice

Be kind.

Even if

They aren't your kind.

Meditate.

Let those thoughts

Simmer and marinate.

Breathe.

Inhale

along with the breeze.

Create.

Before the moment

is too late.

never felt

I've never felt

so alive.

My plants seem to thrive.

I don't eat

things that've died.

All my worst days

I've survived.

Lord knows

I've done nothing but tried.

For this

I am grateful

for I am so alive.

OUTRO

me, my self & the moon

The moon

and me

are one in the same.

      You see the sun

      through the moon.

            You can see God

            through me.

About the Author:

Carrington was born and raised in Danville, Virginia. She is a graduate of the University of Virginia with her bachelor's degrees in African American & African Studies and Philosophy. She got started writing poetry at a young age at her alma mater Carlisle School and was encouraged to continue to write by her English teacher Susan Aaron. This collection of poetry was written over a 2 year period of time from UVA to post graduation by consistently being inspired by life all around her. She now resides in the mountains of central Virginia, where she can be found teaching yoga, eating vegan food, dog sitting and tending to her increasing number of houseplants when not writing.